Meanderings

of a Dark and Lonely Cycle Path

(er…um… Psychopath)

Randy D. Rubin

Portsmouth, VA

Published by Randy D. Rubin

Portsmouth, Virginia
www.dreadmere.com

All Rights Reserved

Edited by Charles H. Fuller, Jr.

Cover Designed by: Charlie Chaplain

Book Design:
Randy D. Rubin
Charles H. Fuller, Jr.

This is a work of fiction. All events, names, persons, and places are a product of my meandering imagination. Any similarities to anyone or anything living, dead, or undead is purely coincidental.

No part of this book may be reproduced in any form by any means without permission, in writing, from the author. The sole exception is by a reviewing party who may quote short passages for the review.

First Edition

ISBN: 978-0-9992041-0-8

Library of Congress Control Number:

Printed in the United States of America

Meanderings

of a Dark and Lonely Cycle Path

(er…um… Psychopath)

Randy D. Rubin

Other works by Randy D. Rubin

E-Book Novellas:

    The Legend of My Nana, Miss Viola

    The Witch of Dreadmere Forest

Collections:

    The Demon in My Head Doth Speak

    The Prison Compendium

Dedication:

This collection of my poetry is lovingly dedicated to the two women
in my life
who have showered me with a lifetime of their love
and made me the proudest man alive.
They are as different as Night and… Marshmallow crème,
Apple and Avocado,
Heaven and the DMV.
They have blessed me
and driven me to lunacy.
These two wonderful women make my flavorless "mash potato
flakes",
hum-drum life complete.
They are Cayenne Pepper and Honey.
They are Cinnamon and Sea Salt.
They are steak sauce and chocolate syrup.
They are my whiskey on the week-ends
and my ice water during the work week.
They are the only two of literally billions of humans to call me dad.
I love my Shawndall DeLyn and my Brandy Cheyenne creatures.
Always have… always will.

Acknowledgements

First and foremost, I want to thank GOD for guiding my hand and giving me this ever-flowing fountain of ideas, these delightful snippets of storylines, character voices and scenic descriptors that gush out of my brain every single day, as well as the precious commodity of time to write these entertainments for you each morning, and the motivation and discipline to write even on those days when I'd rather stream movies and foreign crime drama series, or listen to everything from Led Zepplin, Pink Floyd, ELP and Jethro Tull to Rascal Flatts, Pink and Dan Fogelberg's music or read everyone else's latest horror genre work. As Julie Andrews once sang, "These are a few of my favorite things ... "

Next, I want to thank my wonderful daughters whom I love more than life itself, Shawndall DeLyn and Brandy Cheyenne, for all their continuous unwavering love and support as I pursue my dream. Without them I would not have had the "guts" to submit any of my stories and poetry to the various publishers and editors in the genre for the purposes of entertainment and reading enjoyment.

I'd also like to thank David E. Cowen, Linda D. Addison, and my HWA mentor Paul Dale Anderson for their sage advice and poetic expertise in the making of this collection.

Finally, I'd like to thank my "brother and *compadre* from another *madre*," Charles H. Fuller, Jr., one of the most brilliant, talented and compassionate men I have ever had the privilege of calling my friend. He helped me get this dark poetry collection out to you all. He is a godsend and a wonderful friend. His diligence, perseverance and enthusiasm for this project sometimes seemed to surpass mine and for that invaluable contribution he will get the first copy of this collection. When I say he earned it, trust me, he earned it.

And Thank You, readers of Dark Poetry, for picking this up and reading my book.

Table of Contents

Frost on the Newel Post

Flowers on a Soldier's Grave

The Wire

Dead Canaries

Again Whiskey, Really?

I'm Home

Stirring

That's the Beauty of the Beast

This Garden of Eaten

Wakey Wakey!

Then Scare Me This All Hallows Eve!

Cryposo Woods in the Moonlight

Windy Whispers

The Rope is Gonna Snap!

Her Last Kiss Left on Silver Flute

Down!

The Melancholy Brothers and the Good Dr. Morose

Chasing the Renegade Unicorn

Sit Down and Eat (5 Haikus)

One Hell

Death Bed Confessin'

New Poet's Treason

Poetringles

Praying at Saint Tavern's Cathedral

Any Last Words?

Again…

Silent Agonies of Cherry Pie a La Mode

A Pocket full of Mumblings

Cheesesteak Cheesecake Cheese Plate Cheap
   Date Cheapskate (A Tongue Twister)

To Taste the Nectar of your Kiss (A Triolet)

Like   Comment   Share

Drowning in an Ocean of Ice Cream Soup

Subwaste – Eat Death

Pork Pie Stetson Pete

No, Honestly, Thanks!

Cayenne Pepper and Smoke (A Sonnet)

You Son of a Bitch, You Shot My Dog!

The Wolf Wind

Up!

And Time Marches On

Hot Shrapnel Pie

For Thee I Live

MEANDERINGS

Frost on the Newel Post

There's frost on the newel post,

wet footprints headed up the stair.

A cold wind rushes past you

as if someone is really there.

Faint sobbing in the attic;

a creaking, freaking rocking chair.

This taunting curiosity

that raises up your hackle hair

and causes teeth to chatter

or face to pale of blood.

The piercing screams that shatter

glass—an auditory flood.

Soft weeping past the cellar door

and whispers in the darkened gloom

that change to cackled laughter

when you trod steps down to your doom.

The door is shut tight, wedged and bolted

with a heavy iron lock and hasp

and one would swear there is no air

around that door, you hitch and gasp.

Some music in the parlor

from an old Victorian harpsichord

plays faintly, ever daintily

though there is no such keyboard.

The sounds of children giggling

grows louder then soon fades away

as you pass by the bedroom door

where once they filled their days with play.

Then something from the mantle falls

and shatters at your back.

A bolt of lightning flashes

and the thunderous stormy sky goes, "Crack!"

Kaboom, gone in an instant,

the room returns to sable

as you feel around the darkened room

and bump into a bedside table

filled with gaudy perfume bottles

and medicines galore.

There were potions, balms and lotions.

There were salves and pills and so much more,

but fumbling for the exit

you grope the wall around the bed,

send tumbling a ball, you think

and then you see the severed head.

You scream and run, you nearly faint.

You stumble down the slippery stair.

You trip over a headless corpse

that you'd swear, previously, wasn't there.

The floor is wet and sticky

but you push up to your knees and stand

assisted by a strong arm

who offers you a helping hand

but when you turn to thank him

for aiding your escape

there is no other standing there;

just you with mouth agape.

So you scan the room for exits

and head fast, for the door

as terror drains your blood

until you just can't handle anymore.

A hatchet handle hits you

thrown somewhere from behind.

It very nearly splits you

but Fate is being over-kind.

At last you see the threshold

and you quickly twist the knob.

Run weeping out that haunted house

as grateful for your life, you sob.

But fear and horror push you on

down porch steps running, off you flee

to put a healthy distance

between you and evil destiny.

There's cold frost on these newel posts

as freezing breeze through willows wheeze

and running blindly from the ghosts

you hide in safety midst the trees.

Flowers on a Soldier's Grave

This sad sepulchral ghost's parade

is marching past, this cavalcade of gravestones,

this masquerade of dead flesh and dry bones

forms up a mighty tattoo

stepping left-right-left… right through me

they all marched right up to me, see

and cried.

They ride the light breezes

with tauntings of rifle and bayonet teases

of soft whispered glories implied

and stories of old

filled with honors untold,

glorified

with these flowers, all splayed

in a messy cascade

o'er the graves of the brave

men and women who died…

The Wire

We'll go over it again

until I think you've got it down.

There's a lot of lives at stake

and we really want to nail this clown.

So once more from the top

while I tape the mike in place.

You walk in there just like normal

with your luscious lipstick smile and face

the window. Get him talking;

Have him fix you both a drink.

Sit across from him, relax and

don't let him for a moment think

we're on to him. He'll kill you

in the blinking of an eye.

It's been said he smells a wire

so you'll need to closely watch the guy.

He's as dangerous as burning snakes

and cold as witch's fire.

You can't afford to make mistakes

so keep your wits as things transpire.

Go easy on the alcohol

and keep the music way down low.

Remember not to hug or dance.

Speak clearly—very calm and slow.

He likes his women coy but sharp,

alluring dames with loads of class.

Just play him like a poker game

and mark his cards; expect his pass.

But keep him talking; make him sing.

His song we'll need as evidence

to lock this monkey in a cage

without a moment's hesitance.

If it goes down and goes down wrong

the code word is your ticket out.

We've SWAT team snipers everywhere.

They'll plug this guy. I have no doubt.

But just in case this derringer

you strap on to your gartered thigh

and if you need it use the gun

in the event we miss the guy.

He's killed at least a hundred men

that we can trace. Some with their wives.

They say he even killed the kids.

Asleep, he came and stole their lives.

Be careful and remember that

we're right outside in unmarked vans.

We get this hit man from New York

and you get to make your new life plans.

Dead Canaries

Ya better hold your

fuckin' tongue, son,

if you're talkin' 'bout my Daddy!

That man has worked

in two coal mines;

You better be damned glad he

doesn't come around

that corner, Boy,

and whoop your skinny

bony ass

for thinkin'

whilst a drinkin'

he and me would take that bullshit sass.

For years he worked them double shifts

that kept five young-uns fed and dressed

and now he's got the Black Lung deep

in both sides of his chest

so ya bess be treadin' lightly, Boy,

when Daddy's name comes out your mouth.

You understand my meanin' friend?

(this is where your head

bobs North and South.)

There's four of us replaced him

so he might find some restin' peace.

Our sister now looks after him

and helps him battle that disease

'cause mines are mighty dangerous holes

where dead canaries don't tell lies

they's many a way o' killin' you, Boy,

without no need of alibis.

Again Whiskey, Really?

The moon seems amused

with those sinister, shit-eating grin beams

abused 'gainst a blue-black sky

all battered black and blue and bruised,

smiling down on my drunk ass.

These nasty punk-ass, no class stars

twinkling.

Ice cubes tinkling in my whiskey glass...

got me to thinkling...

'bout how much drinkling

I'm a do

tonight.

All right?

'cause when I'm done, by God,

I'm thu.

They ain't gone be none after this.

No fond fare-thee-well, and no giddy gimme good-night kiss

at the door...

Fuck it! One more, what the hell...

Then I'll get my drunk ass up and take me a piss.

I'm Home

"Morning"

When first we met you wouldn't say a word.

I looked absurd or so I'd overheard but

you smiled at me; your eyes locked onto mine

and in my mind I whispered to myself, "I'm Home."

So two lives thrived and intertwined like Ivy vines

then climbed up to the heavens like a mighty rope

to find some holy blessing and the hope to tie the knot

one day,

or better, right there on the spot!

Your voice, to me, a songbird's morning melody

laced with rink-tink-tinkling fairy bells

and soothing summer waves and ocean swells. My darling dear,

your laughter in my ear is like a love potion so potent

filled with magic happy tears and joyful cheers dusted

with cinnamon and dunked in elderberry wine, and Honeydew.

I close my eyes and pinch my nose and think of you

and there it goes…

A medicine so fine I'd surely die without my daily dose.

If not dead, surely close.

"Afternoon"

"I'm Home!" I yell.

I sniff some sour nasty smell.

I need a half an hour, maybe less

to decompress.

Would I like a cold beer? Why, hell yes!

These three kids try to tackle me as I set down my keys

and 'pretty please' is all I hear

amidst the shouting and the questions and a bottle of cold beer.

Go finish Spelling homework then.

Do what your mother tells you. No, all I have's a ball point pen.

It has to be a pencil. Go take the dog outside.

You're pulling down my trousers son. Let go of Daddy's leg. I tried

to pull away from grabby kids and find a place to sit

when my oldest pushed the baby down and my other, middle child got hit.

Is it too late to quit this 'daddy' shit?

And then you start in with your stories

of your morning chores and your 'morning glories'

boring me toward distant shores

pulled back to your story of hardwood floors

and grocery stores and… and… and…

every minute of your morning

recreated, enervated, and I've waited

for the last two-minute warning of this game.

Aggravated when eventually accentuated

with air quotes and hints of sour notes

and tales of this little one's toy boats

afloat. His vast armada

bouncing G.I. Joes and Popeye's nose in the PP water

splashing about with your toddler daughter

in our toilet

and if you guess the ending please don't spoil it.

We're havin' salmon. Should I bake or broil it?

There's a meeting with the PTA,

and our son's 'an Orange' in his school play;

we've a conference next Tuesday

with his teacher…

tried rescheduling, couldn't reach her.

Movie's got a double feature with some slimy alien creature.

Janice told me Jackie said

that Sally heard that this guy Fred

had mentioned something 'bout a shed

for free.

I said I'd see

if you… if me and you… if maybe we…

And on and on infinity!

Your voice is my insanity!

It never stops! It never ceases,

to amaze me,

though it slowly drives me crazy.

"Evening"

It's cold out!

And somehow, somewhere, somewhen we grew old about

a lifetime-and-a-half ago

after a really nifty fifty swiftly soaring years

(Notice I didn't say boring years?)

together, you and I, you know

forever, you and I, you know…

despite this wicked malady, you know… me,

even though you cannot show me…

anymore.

Or speak my name or

say a single word

or tell me who's to blame or

what you've heard

or bring me 'morning glories',

those delightful little stories of your day

that I'd dismiss and let drift away

and interrupt with kisses

on the sweet lips of my Missus… YOU! God, I miss you!

One whispered word would throw me for a loop,

my lovely hen in this antiseptic chicken coop.

The nurse said you finally took a good poop today.

Yay! What more can I say?

That's one less load off my tired mind.

I come here every day to find you

sitting in this stupid chair – remind you

I'll always be there behind you

every minute that I can, My Love.

I've always been YOUR man, My Love.

Together we have shared a life;

shared love and children, pain and strife

and through it you've remained my wife

despite this terrible disease

that steals you from me by degrees

against my teary heartfelt pleas

on these old wobbly bended knees

as teardrops race down my parchment face

I kneel beside you in this quiet place

And softly weep

Until at last you fall asleep.

"I'm home!"

Stirring

Shhh! Stirring… in the leaves out there!

Hush my sweet and hear

the whispering winds a-stirring

all around us. (Where no one's ever found us!)

Lay quiet with me on this forest floor

while once more, whistling breezes

through the whirring

whirlwinds whip around our heads.

You're almost dead… because I just said so.

So slow you show

your words are slurring

and your wide, wild, whiny child-like eyes

locked in that stare are blurring –

still twinkling in the Autumn moonlight though.

I'll take you slowly, taste your crimson lips

as my claws rip and test the flesh

from breast and chest down to your hips.

I slice them off and toss them in you.

Lick your juices, slick, from sticky fingertips.

I feed. You heard, right, that I had that need?

See, you were warned

but scorned the warning, "Stay inside! Don't leave 'til morning."

You refused to heed it.

Now you bleed; your guts are freed

so I may feed.

You were told when not to go, but no! The words were wasted,

so sure you were of when to go.

Now I the lonely Wendigo

must feast, must dine and finish what I've tasted,

opened up and warm blood basted.

I care not for your soul.

I care more for your belly hole.

You are my shredded body bowl

of innards stew.

I roar for more of you,

my sloppy soup! My steaming pile of bloody gloop

and coils of cool intestine loop.

You must be cooling

as I'm drowning, and in you, I'm drooling

watching while your blood is pooling

I'm ensuring,

as does the beast,

a culinary feast

or hearty meal, to say the least

but first your insides I keep…stirring.

That's the Beauty of the Beast

Come setting sun, while everyone has gone their separate way.

The Beast is waiting silently to stalk its weary prey.

The Hunter and the Hunted will be present at the feast,

but the table's only set for one—that's the beauty of the Beast.

The drinks, the laughs, the epitaphs they write in their heads—Stones.

They play their games of Lust and Found in whispered undertones.

"Don't I know you from somewhere, Babe?"

"Yeah Love, you're my parish priest… but I won't tell if you won't."

That's the beauty of the Beast.

Another drink, you try to think on how much you have spent.

The Beast just stole your wallet, took the cash and out the door he went.

All clues lead to the urinals where what's purchased is just leased

and you shake on the agreement. That's the beauty of the Beast.

"All right, last call for alcohol, then all o' ya'll get out!"

"The Beast has kept you here too long." You hear the barkeep shout.

"Drink up, I'm closed." "I'm open now!" as palms get heavily 'greased'

to keep the whisky flowin'. That's the beauty of the Beast.

Now in the car, not going too far, just up the street and off to bed.

You're locked in mortal combat with the Beast inside your sleepy head.

It pulls your eyelids down then "Bump!" The fender's slightly creased.

Insurance ought to cover it. That's the beauty of the Beast.

The sirens wail, the lights, the jail they lock you in till dawn.

They haul you out next morning but the Beast is somehow gone.

You hit a pregnant woman. We hold both now as deceased.

For a while we thought the baby… That's the beauty of the Beast.

The lawyers show, post bail, you go. They set the dates for court.

They set you free to meet the Beast again. Give your report

to your drinking friends and buddies; Let them know you were released

on a minor technicality… That's the beauty of the Beast.

This Garden of Eaten

Go on, take a bite!

I am both the apple

and the serpent.

You took my Eve from me

while she slept;

while I stepped

outside this unholy, undead place,

this Garden of Eaten

and I wept.

In a single day my life has changed:

You bit her in the morning

and she turned to rotted fruit,

forbidden fruit, by afternoon.

In twilight there was no more Eve.

No more Eve-nings spent with her in paradise—

Only darkest, undead night.

Go on, take a bite

of my Adam's apple.

Join me in this Garden of Eaten.

Wakey Wakey!

Wakey! Wakey! Hands off snakey.

Hey! Wrong person... big mistakey!

Never touch me, never shakey!

Get out now or face I'll breakey.

One more hour of sleep I'm takey

or YOUR body will be achey.

Go away now! Goodness sakey!

Breakfast and some coffee makey—

Croissants maybe, hot and flakey,

buttered grits with eggs and bacey.

Maybe a piece of coffee cakey.

THEN come back and Wakey! Wakey!

Then Scare Me This All Hallows Eve!

Hey you! Hey Bum, get up I said.

Go on now, get on out of here!

This ain't no stinking hotel bed.

The alley's got to be kept clear.

It's Halloween; go scare someone.

Go find a bench out near the park.

I'll call the cops if aren't gone

or kick your tail here in the dark.

        Okay, all right. I'm getting up.

        Don't call the cops. I'm leaving now.

        Just let me get my hat and cup

        and paper bag. Don't drop a sow.

        It's cold out on this Autumn night:

        I just stopped here to rest a while.

        I know I look a sore eyes sight

        Amidst your stylish garbage pile.

You'd do well to move on now, Tramp.

I've said all that I care to say.

Go find yourself another camp,

for in my alley you'll not stay.

        I never meant to frighten you.

        I'm really not as I appear.

        A vagabond I seem, that's true.

        Allow me Sir, to make this clear.

        I am a teller of great tales.

        A writer, Sir, with mighty pen

        but meager were my published sales

        and profits fell time and again.

Perhaps a yarn you'd spin for me.

I've almost finished locking up.

A shocker full of tragedy

would earn your meal and fill your cup.

Come in and wash then, Sagaman.

A tale of evil, I believe

is quite in order. If you can,

then scare me this All Hallows Eve!

Cryposo Woods in the Moonlight

A hint of a glint of a moonbeam kissed
the wings of those things in the midnight mist.
While they loop and they spin and they flutter about
to the cricket's chirp and the bullfrog's shout.
The dragonflies hover to cover their dance
and might join in, given half a chance.
The weeping willows sway in the breeze
waving "come on over" to the other trees
where the hoot owls hoot and the bats hang out
and the wolves unpack and the vultures pout.
There's a creeping crawler and slithering snake
and a lumbering giant thing, makes the ground quake.
The moon is their spotlight, the dark woods, their stage.
The night tells their story without one turned page.
There are quicksands where bone hands reach up towards the sky
and under that boulder, a beast with one eye
tries to grab at your shoulder, or grasp for your throat
and rip out your screams before the second note.
A tentacled mass makes a pass and constricts
wrapping suction cup suckers, more pain it inflicts
as it feeds in the weeds on its unwary prey
then slithers back to its swamp, hidden away.
The howlers and growlers are out on the prowl
while perched on its bough sits the night watchman owl
who wonders aloud each character's name
so later he'll have some idea who to blame

for the ca-daver curtain calls, dead body bows,

the carrion curtsies rigor mortis allows.

A slight touch too much of the vines in the wood

that entwine round your ankles and tangle up good

while the thorns and the briars, the nettles and burrs

prickling pokes at your skin 'til the burning occurs

and the itching and twitching and stinging begin.

Red rashes and welts start to blister your skin

but you can't scratch your itches, the vines wrap your wrists,

encircling your body with loops and tight twists

that cause you to swell up and blister and bleed

while you think that a scratching is all that you need,

but the vines climb your torso and more so, your throat;

make a red blistered necklace to match your neck bloat.

You don't hear the noise when the poison takes hold.

The swell and the smell of you, best left untold.

The moon very soon hides it pale face in shame.

Cryposo, at midnight has death in its name.

There's fur on the brambles and blood in the moss

from creatures whose features no one's come across,

like that huge hairy hump back with leathery wings

and scales on both tails with those hard, spikey things.

Or that lady that soars through the night darkened sky

with the three rows of teeth and the third glowing eye,

screaming curses and cuss words and people's first names

like she's constantly livid at those whom she blames.

We've that two-headed imp with the really big feet
and his sister, Miss Twister whose breath smells so sweet
like a fresh batch of cookies all warm and delicious
but don't get too close 'cause she's really quite vicious.
She bit through the neck of the last one too close;
chewed off half of an ear and both lips and a nose.
The clouds wrap their shrouds round the shivering moon
and the night snuggles in, for the dawn's coming soon
so they slide in and hide in the darkness, the lairs,
or the caves, under rocks, in the trees, 'neath your stairs
or under the water or under the ground
they hide quietly without making a sound.
They wait for the night and the light of the moon
that they know will return and return very soon.

Windy Whispers

Wispy wintry clouds,

those great grey flannel shrouds

crowd the night sky in gloom

backing out of their starry room

silently,

on tiptoe, in woolen sock feet

leaving soon

as the sugar cookie moon

with one bite bitten off

shines its pallid light softly

frosting, with icing, the tree tops

that sway to the tune of the breeze

with its gentle gypsy squeeze box breaths.

Midnight moonlight melody mocks Death and rocks

the boughs back and forth,

to and fro, half froze they wish to doze while music so morose

 so very rhythmic, sweet and slow.

Lyrics only the last leaves know;

lull-a-byes up to the sleepy skies… sung in windy whispers.

The Rope is Gonna Snap!

"The rope is gonna snap!" he yells

as he shoots straight up out of bed.

The strands are frayed and wires exposed;

He tries to grab them in his head.

"The rope is gonna snap!" he cries

but no one is around to hear

the humming thrum of line stretched taut.

The splitting twang rings crystal clear.

"The rope is gonna snap!" he screams.

He hangs suspended by a thread

of sanity. His rope-burned grasp

is slipping into abject dread.

"The rope is gonna snap!" he laughs.

There is no reason to hang on.

If he succumbs now to the fear

then quicker it will all be gone.

"The rope is gonna snap!" he prays

for God to save him from this fate.

He can't hold on much longer now.

"Please Lord, show me I'm not too late."

And when he let loose of all hope

he found

he held

another

rope…

Her Last Kiss Left on Silver Flute

She tried to learn to play the flute

for me.

Her crippled melodies were cute.

She'd play incessantly

to see

just how astute

I'd be

and catch her fractured rhapsody

in names dispute.

She died and left her silver flute

to me;

Those crystal memories are mute.

She lives for all eternity

inside of me,

you see.

I can't refute

her death, a senseless tragedy.

My tears dilute

her last kiss, left on silver flute…

Down!

Down into the darkness,

Step *down* on every cellar stair

The whispers *down* the bottom, black

Are calling you *down* further where

The ghosts roam moaning *down* cold halls

Of ochre-colored stones, groaning *down* sepulchral holes

                         and crooked cracks and weeping walls.

Onward still you follow, try swallowing *down* your fears.

Your mouth dries out, something cries out; *down* further still

       a ghost appears.

You jump against the slimy stones and slide *down*

     to your wobbly knees

The lone ghost floats o'er old, cold bones, goes *down*

your throat despite your pleas.

The Melancholy Brothers
and the Good Doctor Morose

I was plopped down on a park bench

with my hoodie pulled 'round me close

'cross from the melancholy brothers

and the good Doctor Morose.

The hawk was blowin' high notes

that caused this drippin' from under my nose.

Doc said he couldn't feel

his lips, his fingers or his pinky toes

as the brothers Melancholy

popped the tops on bags of beer near froze

and shared a pair of gloves turned orange

from munching on some stale Cheetos.

They danced the sidestep sidewalk shuffle.

(Akesthesia I suppose.)

These ballerina polar bears

with shit stains on their clothes.

"How about them fuckin' Redskins, man?"

"That quarterback tossed some crazy-ass throws."

"They sacked that jack-off three damn times!"

"Those worthless so-and-so's."

Then Doc pulls out a cherry blunt

and fired up a flaming cherry rose.

The brothers Melancholy blocked the hawk

and stopped their two-step tap dance shows.

"Check out that fat bitch over there."

"She's one dem freaky-deaky hoes

that got a closet full of leather shit

and a nightstand full of black dildoes."

"Don't laugh, that chick is bankin' cash.

That's how that mighty river flows.

She keeps that bank roll safely stashed.

How 'bout passing back my blunt, there, Bros!"

The beer can bags are their basketballs

and Mel drinks for the semi-pros.

His brother, Choly, blocks his shot.

These quibbling sibling, sniveling foes.

Then the silence pulls our zippers up

and the hawk starts trumpeting "Tally-hos"

That sugar frost noiseless snowflakes,

on the heads of us quiet Eskimos.

The Melancholy brothers

and the good Doctor Morose

are standing in the winter chill

blowing blunt smoke Cheerios.

The Doc is leaving to eat his gun.

Why his wife had to die, heaven knows.

But he can't keep going on like this;

Watch the love of his life, in their bed, decompose.

"Think I'll go to my girlfriend's on Dreadmere Street

Make some noodles and watch cooking shows."

(If that bitch screams "Please untie me!" once more,

we'll probably come to blows!)

Soon his brother will leave for his mama's house.

(Choley likes dressing up in her clothes.)

Especially the way that her silk stockings feel

with her seven-inch platform stilettos.

But for now, we're just wandering vagabonds

come to palaver, drink, juxtapose,

share a blunt, fart, tell jokes, and talk football

dressed like four drunken thrift store scarecrows.

Then the doc climbs up his walking cane

stands up, stretches, salutes and then goes,

while the brothers rummage for pocket change

and the darkness around us grows.

Mel's nose is running down over his lip

and his teeth look like chewed Oreos

that are chittering chattering vibrating cold

but thems the least of his fuckin' woes.

I reckon its time I find somewhere to sleep.

That orange creamsickle light, overhead, softly glows.

This park bench is finally snow covered white

as am I, so I guess that its time that I rose

and bid my farewells to the brothers

Mel and Choley, two beer bag buffalos

when a gunshot sounds off in the distance

near the house of the good Doc Morose.

We hear sirens off in the distance

getting shriller and louder and close.

They speed past the park where we're standing.

Three snow-crusted half-froze hobos.

There's a wash machine box by the beer store

hid behind the stacked-up milk crate rows

that should keep out the hawk, and the snow off my face

while I'm taking my evening's repose.

In the morn, if the Good Lord will wake me

and I haven't been completely froze

I'll grab me a hot breakfast biscuit

and a bottle of wild Irish rose,

then head back to my bench with my buddies-

The beer can bag breakfast club Bros.

to sit there and watch as the world passes by

and live out the life that we chose.

Chasing the Renegade Unicorn

Round and round, and up and down this daily carousel revolves

as Horror Horses set the pace

they race

and the renegade Unicorn gives chase, evolves,

breaks off his bondage pole, his very soul at last runs free.

The soundtrack racetrack, whip crack symphony,

played pipes and horns, calliope

and children's laughter filled with glee,

chasing happily ever after

on the heels of that magnificent beast

who tramples clouds off to the east;

trails rainbows as it gallops off.

The Tigers and the Zebras scoff.

They can't keep up; they wheeze and cough

while stripping prison stripes they try to doff

and find a place to hide their hides,

exposing their insides

(and broken poles)

as Lions pass them with their prides.

A Pegasus flies overhead

to signal the Carousel is dead

or dying at the very least.

The Brass Ring chase, that chariot race has finally ceased,

bereft of jungle animals or beast

equine, feline, porcine, canine.

They're all gone, they've run off—that's fine.

Chasing that renegade Unicorn

who calls them to arms with his magical horn

and leads them to charge towards each new sunlit morn.

Sit Down and Eat (5 Haiku)

Sit down and finish.

Your dinner's getting colder

than frozen Grandma,

rockin' in her chair,

icicles in her white hair.

Frozen matriarch

heard Grandpa out there

on the front porch swing, singing

tunes of love for her

even though he's dead

now nigh on twenty-two years.

No more frozen tears,

so sit down and eat.

You ain't getting no older,

food's getting colder.

One Hell

There is but one Hell

with vistas various,

with charred and blackened areas,

and landscapes lush and panoramic views

both darkness drenched and filled with vibrant hues

existing on the maps of our own mind

where meandering, we wander with our eyes

open wide, yet oblivious and blind,

with silent screams and stifled cries

continually lost

and no idea the actual cost

to ask directions

as there are no intersections

because there is but one Hell,

under God, indivisible,

believable yet still invisible.

Inconceivable as far as anyone can tell

because

we are but one Hell.

Death Bed Confessin'

Papaw's evidently dyin'; least that's what Memaw just said.

And he wants to put some things to right while he's still right in the head.

Told Memaw he wants you and me to bury him 'hind the shed,

after he gets done confessin' to us both from his death bed.

So go get your goll damn boots on and go warm up the truck.

We's fittin' to go to Papaw's house and listen to the old fart cluck…

and find my favorite camo hat with the little eider duck.

Seems he means to grab my last good nerve and give it one last pluck.

Go on now make some coffee, Son, and call me when it's done.

He better be dyin' this damn time; I'm shaky, and I ain't the one

to drive round these misty mountains till we meet the morning sun

just to listen to some bullshit from a man who lived life on the run.

He thinks we don't know nothin' 'bout his whiskey makin' skill

or the secret place back in them woods where he hides his whiskey still.

He don't realize that you and I'se been sneakin' up that hill

for nigh on thirteen years and drinking up his sour mash swill.

Got my java in the thermos and the six-pack cooler's packed

with some samiches of deer meat all wrapped and neatly stacked.

Now go and kiss your maw goodbye, Son, before your head gets whacked

and put my pistol in the truck just in case we get attacked.

You're sittin' there beside me in the truck but haven't said a word.

Your Papaw might be dyin' boy, in case you haven't heard.

I personally believe my Daddy dyin's just a tad absurd.

He's just mostly hard of hearin' and his vision's getting blurred

from all that whisky he been cookin' up for nigh on fifty-seven years,

and the wood smoke and the reefer, and the cigarettes and beers,

and the hoochie-mama chasin', and fightin' all them queers

and at the end it starts to slip away, his memory disappears.

We're here now Son, go quietly and give Memaw a great big squeeze

and kiss her on the cheek and be as pleasant as you please.

We'll join her on the porch; take a minute with this mountain breeze,

then we'll mozy up to Papaw's room and get down on our bended knees and find out what them secrets are the old man needs off of his chest

so he can go on ahead and die and get to heaven's peaceful rest.

My maw looks like this might be it and Memaw knows the old man best.

She went and called the preacher and got Papaw Sunday dressed.

I'm a go up first, alone boy, hear his damn death bed confessin'

and I'll call y'all up afterward; they's family things that needs addressin'

then we'll gather round his bedside and we'll hear the preacher's blessin'

and if he ain't dead by sun-up Son, go fetch my trusty Smith and Wesson.

New Poet's Treason

You've committed the heinous, unspeakable crime

of harboring poetry with the intent to rhyme

for some ungodly reason we don't understand!

You've got so many words at your command

yet you refuse to use them the way we've deemed fit.

Your poems all have meter and structure and wit;

They have cadence and accents, coherence and plottin'.

They use alliteration and big words we've forgotten.

You've made quintuplet couplets iambic and fun,

you've designed various stories; entertained everyone

but there's only so much of this word rhyming writing.

It's frighteningly 'old school' and rather exciting

but I'm sent to arrest you for crimes 'gainst insanity.

Your piss-poor excuses for poems and profanity,

inciting smirks with your rhyming word quirks

while Poem Police jerks in their new 'lines of works'

write fresh tickets/citations/slanted line demarcations/

that clearly speak 'poem'/at most Poem Police stations.

So show me your hands now and put down that pen

and don't make me say what I've just said again.

You're a dangerous poet, a threat to us all.

Your poems are just indecent, hack, chicken scrawl.

You are under arrest now for crimes, rhyme and reason,

and charged with committing the new poet's treason.

You have the write
to remain
stifled. Is this pen loaded?
If I check in your
pockets will I be pricked
or cut
or ink stained?
Anything you say or write,
however trite
can and will
be used
against you.
You have the write to a
Thesaurus.
If you cannot afford
one...

Poetringles

One hundred thirteen wicked words
and three 'drama' commas
stacked on top of one another
like those salt-covered
chips that are neither potato
or pine bark
or autumn dried oak leaves
that resemble sour cream and onion
or mesquite barbeque flavored duck lips
strangely arranged
in a tubular tower of
transparent transfiguration
from the inherent reality
of one carefully crafted
complex sentence
into the magical
realm of a
shared supercilious
and mutually perceived
piece of post hypnotic hypocrisy,
a sculpture chiseled from the finest
wordsmith wood, finely crafted
and polished to perfection
and sold to the highest bidder
by some snickering gyp,
some swindling diddler
who calls this long sentence statue…
poetry.

Praying at Saint Tavern's Cathedral

Bless me compadre for I have chagrinned,

I may have sinned;

I just broke wind. (Heh heh Heh)

I'll take my seat at this multi-stooled

(Oops, I think I drooled)

Leather-covered and hand-tooled

Confessional.

Don't try thish at home; I'm a pour fresh and all.

I'm a pro-fession-al.   (there it goes)

I'm a walking funeral processional

so pour me a fresh un, Al.

Be a mother fuckin' Pal.

Bloody Mary, she's my gal.

She never fucked around on me

like my ex-wife did after thirty-three

years (L'Chaim) to life… for reasons of uncertainty.

If I'd only had a knife or gun (or piece of gum)

I'd end this pain and have some fun

Can I get an amen… from anyone?

Who's that good-looking sinner in the mirror?

My eyes ain't seein' any clearer

but tell him he looks like Richard Gere or

George Clooney, maybe,

or Clint Eastwood in Million Dollar Baby…

…long after Misty told him, "Play me".

What the fuck you lookin' at dude

with your devil-may-care attitude

and your persnickety, piss-poor platitude.

Oh, and speaking of pissing and pouring

there, friend. Your sermon is rather boring.

See? The padre's damn near snoring.

Pour me another while I piss,

please Padre, pour and pray that I don't miss.

I'm usually quite good at this

so bless me with another round.

No sermon on the mount or mound.

Go placidly, mouth, without a sound.

Hail Marys of the blood,

I Noah guy who likes this kind of flood.

(I'm talkin' about myself there, Bud)

I've paid my penance and said my prayer

and given my money to the guy over there

with the bar rag cassock and the icy stare.

Our father, who works this sacred bar

I followed the light of your neon star

to Saint Tavern's Cathedral from afar.

I'm not here for your righteous indignation

I came to confess I need spirits –Libation!

Bloody Mary please ease my tribulation.

It's time I leave so bless my soul.

Here's a sawbuck for your TIPS fish bowl

and keep the quarters for the mints that I stole.

I guess I'll see you around, there, brother.

Give my heartfelt cheek smooch to our mother.

Okay maybe I do have time for another,

but just one more,

and then my happy ass is out that happy hour door.

We've paid this penance once or twice before.

Any Last Words?

You got any last words 'fore I put on this here hood?

Might take ya self a moment and make 'em sound real good

'cause you're 'bout to meet your maker and hear them angels sing.

Once we set your carcass danglin' from this thirteen neck loops thing.

You shouldn'ta went and killed them folk or robbed that dad gum bank

or stole all them there horses. Its only you you've got to thank

for gettin' caught red handed with them aces up your sleeve.

You're slicker'n snowy owl shit with all them moves you learnt to thieve

so gone ahead and speak your piece, unburden your dark soul

for the killin' and the cheatin' and all that gold you stole

and whilest you're beggin' for forgiveness and pleadin' for another chance

remember, Missus Outlaw, about to do the hangman's dance,

that around these parts we's peaceful folk who likes a peaceful life

and we don't take kind to ladies who kills kinfolk with a kitchen knife

and steals their hard-earned propity, their money and their guns,

then runs off with their horses and just runs and runs and runs.

You killed a new born baby, and a preacher and Doc's nurse.

Nobody really gives a hoot which one you think is worse!

So… If you've got any words to say afore I'm 'bout to hang ya,

go on and get 'em spoke and Mama, then you're dead, Goll dang ya!

76

Again…

Again…
with pen
I pierce the virgin membrane
of the page.
Perhaps assuage
the demons of my thoughts –
I think
I'll spill more of their blood –
Black Ink!
And write the line
that brings the eye to tear
or vanquishes man's fear
or causes belly laugh,
maybe an epitaph
that written, will at least
be heard
in one man's mind
where spoken word
is born.

Silent Agonies of Cherry Pie À La Mode

No one hears

the silent screams

of icy cold ice creams

as they weep their French Vanilla tears

seeping into luscious, bloodshot, gooey

cherry eyes.

It's warm good-byes,

and melted, muted cries.

The constant struggling

with its heavy cream load

snuggling its crispy, crunchy, crumbly, crust

as ice cream in its pomp and glory must

be pie a la mode.

The cream tears soak the feathery flakes

that butter, salt and flour makes.

It blinds the cherry children as they, nestled in their blanket,

sleep, perchance to cream with just cause gets its just desserts

and weeps as it dies

atop so many worthy pies.

A Pocket Filled with Mumblings

I've a pocket filled with mumblings,

angry ramblings, muttered grumblings,

buttered fumblings, shuffled stammerings.

Sputtered bumblings, tummy rumblings,

staggered stumblings on this humbling

moonlit night.

Haggard… ambling under tumbling

starry light

and in my dark and dreary fright,

as if what's wrong is really right

has left me trembling…

A Master Sensei's Love in Five Haikus

Take my Tanto knife!

Know who is after you but

now run for your life.

Your enemies come.

They want to know your secrets;

You must act quite dumb.

Go, leave me alone;

I will keep her occupied

so you can escape.

Do not circle back.

She is well versed in this trick

and won't be deceived.

Run far to the East

where the sun rise meets your smile

and the wounds hurt least.

Cheesesteak Cheesecake Cheese Plate
Cheapskate Cheap Date

(My tongue twister!)

Hold on a fuckin' minute! Wait...

You thought I was a cheapskate

after all that fuckin' chow you ate!

You downed a pound of cherry cheesecake,

a fat foot long Philly cheesesteak,

a jumbo choco-mocha milk shake

then you call yourself a cheap date?

You polished off a whole cheese plate.

I think the owner's calling a magistrate.

Maybe I made a huge mistake

and we both need to take a bit of a break.

(Watching you gives me a stomachache!)

Hold on a minute... Wait!

I know it's getting really late

I had a nice time, at any rate.

To Taste the Nectar of Your Kiss
(A Triolet)

To taste the nectar of your kiss

again 'fore battle I must go,

I'd pledge my heart's eternal bliss

to taste the nectar of your kiss.

Wrapped in your arms I'll truly miss

your warm embrace. I've but, you know,

to taste the nectar of your kiss

again 'fore battle I must go.

Like   Comment   Share

Like.
Stunning!
Very pretty.
Yes, you're lovely.
WOW, you look amazing!
Okay you're fucking gorgeous already!
(Where's your fucking husband?)
Really?
Must you fish for
compliments
every-fucking-day?
(why not cast your line using YOUR Hubby's pole?)
(is he tired of your bait, I wonder?)
This book of Face, this social place
your hand-held vanity mirror
showing us your face, or just a trace
(from pictures taken somewhere around 1984)
your lovely smile
(Made of bright white 10,000-dollar veneers,
'Cheers!' Compliments
of YOUR husband)
and your new hair style,
that you change every once in a while.

You, (LIKE!) sitting at your vanity

wanting reassurances of sanity

and beauty. (SHARE!)

You open up your 'vane'

to bleed, to drip and dribble

drops of blood like autumn rain

to cleanse the wound and heal your pain.

(COMMENT!) Like you?

I don't really know enough about you

'cept you (LIKE!) to fish

at the deep end of this pond for shallow compliments.

This secret spot you stand in social safety

'long the banks…

and then you grace us with a royal "THANKS."

HAPPY FACE   HEART   THUMBS UP

Drowning in an Ocean of Ice Cream Soup

I'm drowning in an ocean of ice cream soup
out past the beige capped, foamy root beer waves.
Grasping at straws, gasping strawberry scary truth,
it's hard to stay afloat now days,
from a soda fountain booth.
I float here in this milk and shake.
This ain't no piece of chocolate cake,
I'm whipped, I'm chilly and I'm feeling licked,
fish-lips kissed and fudge tongue flicked
and here's the scoop,
real deal
banana peel, I feel
as if it's time we split.
And all things told
I know that's cold
but I can't handle it.
There's no hot caramel sauces
or butterscotch dips.
No pralines or raisins or mint chocolate chips,
just vanilla bean tears dripping onto my chest
and I'm wishing I hadn't worn my Sundae best.

Subwaste – Eat Death

Hungry?

Have to have a sub to eat.

No Sub-stitute

for foot-long subs with double meat.

It's been so long…

It is so long…

A steak and cheese,

yes, toasted please.

A coupon and a 'Snub Club' card

(Don't make this hard), its easy-peasy

Lemon-pepper Mayo squeazy,

don't you see-zy?

This makes it "buy one get one free"-zy

(with a fountain drink.)

"Not too hard to figure out."

I try hard not to shout… I think.

The 'Snub Club' points on this, my card

you realize, (Don't make this hard!)

could purchase this entire franchise.

Take however much you need

for this transaction to succeed.

A foot-long double meat – proceed.

Sub–ordinate sub-standard stumblebum

and her manager, Punjab Tweedledum

has come to tell me no and no,

and so this so-and-so

says this coupon for the second sub

of equal or lesser value, Bub

cannot be used with 'double meat'

(his language knowledge incomplete)

outside of 'sub' vernacular

and his spreading a bed of shredded lettuce

on fresh bread fetish

IS somewhat spectacular.

But he acts like he can't understand me.

Grr! Why not? Do what? You can't? he tries to reprimand me.

I can't? The coupon clearly states… I rant?

Sub-altern (Don't make this hard!) sub-dolous fool

I know the rule you sub-servient sandwich tool.

Fifteen dollars for a drink?

You've hit some buttons wrong I think.

No you don't understand. Let me explain.

Yes get the manager. This is insane.

I'm seething with rage but I'm quiet and calm

as I squeeze the 'Sub Club' card, cutting my palm

when a beautiful lady behind me in line, being kind,

says that SHE doesn't mind

paying the few dollars more

for the homeless old man's meal so I'll just leave the store.

Ahhhhh! Embarrassment's Dart

has easily gone and pierced my heart.

This sweet young lady I can no longer face

has thrust her kindest dagger in my disgrace

Saying, "I'll pay for the homeless guy"

and I can't even look her in the eye

But in my shame (Don't take this hard!)

I thank her just the same

For her kindness. "You're so very sweet

But I'll go somewhere else to eat."

Then backing out, I turn to leave,

embarrassed like you would not believe.

Black billowy clouds form in my brain;

inside my head this hungry storm of half-baked dread

and I'm about to spread some toasted lead

on a bed of shredded dead and, "You've got insufficient bread so you

can't eat."

A couple footlong double barrel treat

that brings the heat and can't be beat.

Subwaste - Meet death!

Pork Pie Stetson Pete

Pork Pie Stetson Pete

lies face down in the street

and no one says a goddam thing,

just acts like nothing's happening,

no gunshot hittin' the sweet spot

from some hot shot with a bag of pot

and a goose egg on the side of his head

and Pork Pie Stetson Pete on this dirty street lies dead.

And the blood and his brains

trickle into the sewer drains

and nobody says their good-byes

or goes over to close what's left of his eyes

and no one says a goddam thing

just acts like nothing's happening.

Business as usual down on dirty street,

stepping over him, wiping blood off their feet.

Somebody call a cop.

Somebody make that ringing noise stop

from that loud ass pistol blast.

There's a ten-dollar bill in his fist. Grab it fast

then go get a blanket to cover him,

We want the police to discover him.

We don't want to be too close, too involved

but we want to see this mystery solved

of why Pork Pie Stetson Pete

lies face down in the street.

The silence screams conspiracy as it shakes its angry fists

at the pretty city coroner and forensic scientists

who couldn't find their asses with both hands

and a flashlight and a mirror

When the whole thing's right in front of them

and behind them, crystal clear.

Pork Pie Stetson Pete

lies face down in the street

and nobody says a goddam word,

just acts like nothing happened

this whole crime scene thing's absurd,

while his hat becomes a tumbleweed blowing down the boulevard

and later on, his mama gonna take it pretty hard

when they tell her Pork Pie Stetson Pete

is now a chalk line down on dirty street,

where the wind don't seem to give a shit

and the rain just doesn't care

about the five-inch hole, the breakfast bowl

that used to be his skull and hair.

Soon all the shops flip "We're Closed!" signs

and lock their plate glass doors.

It's way past time for Pete's priest and a bit too early for the whores

so Pork Pie Stetson Pete

died face down in the street

and no one says a goddam thing.

No one saw a goddam thing

just acts like nothing's happening.

No, Honestly, Thanks.

Thanks. No, honestly, thanks.
I mean it. Thank you.
I left you in the darkness
to watch over me and keep me safe.
Thank you for that precious rest
and a womblike warmth,
wrapped up against the early morning cold.
I'm getting old so getting up
is getting harder.
Yes, I'm an early riser with a cold plug in my starter
becoming more and more
of less and less
and not remembering what for.
A most appreciated, monumental gift,
this waking up.
This getting out of bed and taking up
the charge again.
This trying to make art with a keyboard and a pen
so thanks for this gift of "every single day".
I can't really think of a better way
except to come right out and say
Thank You, my sweet and precious Lord.
No, Honestly, Thanks.

Cayenne Pepper and Smoke
(A Sonnet)

With a voice of cayenne pepper and smoke,

she sings songs like sauces, savory and sweet.

Her eyes are the color of fresh artichoke

that blaze with a smoldering cooking fire heat.

Her guitar feeds all of these hungry folk

who come really ravenous, ready to eat.

They'd devour up every lyric she spoke

and politely refuse to leave their seat,

as they drink and they laugh at her every joke

and they wave at everyone they meet.

They listen loaded or almost broke

'til we toss them back out to the street.

And when her last sweet song's dessert is done,

she smiles and bows, serves up another one.

You Son of a Bitch, You Shot my Dog!

You son of a bitch, you shot my dog
and now you're gonna pay.
See, that there's the way we roll up here;
us mountain folk don't play.

They's a code we foller up in these parts
And you done cracked a big 'un
So it's only fittin' and proper, Son,
That you gonna do some serious diggin'

'cause somebody got to bury my bitch-
The best blue tick what's ever been
then you gonna dig a second grave
and that un's the hole I'm a bury you in.

You ought not been where the fuck you was
Nor seed what you think you seed
so now you and me's gonna take us a walk
And I'm fittin' to make you bleed.

You son of a bitch, you shot my dog
and they's nary one word to say
that'd keep me from getting' my justice due.
I been done told ya, it's just that way.

So don't even think about runnin'.
They ain't no need to cry, plead or beg.
You go tryin' to jack rabbit off in these woods
I'm a blow off your dad gum leg.

Mama's up fryin' some chicken
and Daddy's out huntin' some big ass deer.
When they catch wind 'bout the buckshot in Blue
Well um… best get your sorry ass in gear.

I reckon you think since you ain't from up here
I might give you a second chance
But we gonna walk twixt them mountains up yonder
And ya'll gonna make that ol' coal shovel dance

'cause you son of bitch, you shot my dog
Keep movin' Son, up this way
Jump over that rotted dogwood log
And take this here time to pray.

That won't my Daddy you saw up there
With the preacher's wife on Widow's Hill
And that won't no Marijuana patch
Growin' other side of that whisky still.

Ain't none of that none of your bizness boy
Ain't nary one bit your affair
And I reckon I'm still a bit wonderin'
What the hell was you doin' up there

And don't try and tell me you's huntin'
I believe you was stalkin' my pa.
You knew he was sweet on the preacher's wife
And was secretly steppin' out on my ma.

You son of a bitch, you shot my dog

The Wolf Wind

The Wolf Wind whirls and whips and howls
as drips of spittle from thundercloud scowls -
send stringy, stinking, stinging storm drops
from its icy tongue that pelts my frigid face.
Rain snarls and guttural growls in thundery gales
of wintry wet warning
where it displays
ferocious fangs filled with fury and freezing spray.
Another frightfully dreary,
dreadfully damp and weary day.

Fellatio Fish Sandwiches

Fellatio fish sandwiches
with a side of hot clenched thighs.
Two tasty juicy bitches
order me up Super-Size
as they peel off skin tight britches,
you can see it in their eyes
that they have soft taco itches
only my burrito satisfies.
I'm not real sure of which is
the winner of my fun meal prize,
but this one's prone to twitches
while her mother shudders, moans, and cries.

Up!

Up!
Climb *up* the slimy, slippery stones.
Just pull *up* out of that pile of bones,
hand over hand, *up* the well's slick wall.
Haul your zombie carcass *up* – Don't fall!
There's that taunting, yellow moon *up* at the very tippy top.
You'll be out that daunting well, *up* haunting soon, if you
    don't drop.
Flesh is rotting off your undead corpse, *up* to your cracked and
    crumbly knees.
Black blood smearing every well stone you reach *up* to,
    inching closer by degrees.
Now at last you hear the wind's song, lifting *up* and over the
    ledge.
Dragging the dregs of your remains, blood stains and veins *up*
    on the stone's edge.

And Time Marches On

I'm frightened now. As
fine folks I've befriended and relatives
whose days have ended
lose their lives like lightning flies
at Autumn's first frost, Winters lost,
violent Vernal tempests tossed
I stand against these gales, waiting with my fingers crossed,
wailing as I weigh the cost
while they leave us without good-byes.
Their souls take flight across the skies
as broken hearts and teary eyes
and silent solitary cries
make memories that remain suspended, then are gone.
And Time wipes the blood from its blade and marches on.
And Time marches on. And time marches…

Hot Shrapnel Pie

How 'bout a nice piece of my Hot Shrapnel Pie?
I think you might just maybe hanker a hunk.
I could make you a plate that'd bring tears to your eye.
Come on, let's break you off a big chunk.

You're tied to your seat; so you might as well eat;
's why I bolted your chair to the floor.
I figured I'd bake you a pie as a treat
that's bursting with goodness and filled with C-4,

with magnesium cheesium melting on top,
every tidbit just melts on your tongue
while explosions of flavor deliciously pop
and make you feel forever young.

So fire up those taste buds for Hot Shrapnel Pie.
You'll be screaming this dessert's "the bomb!"
The best (and the last) treat that you'll ever try.
So tasty you might go and bitch slap your mom.

For Thee I Live

For Thee I live
to learn and love Your precious Word
and yearn for more, Dear Lord.
The days you fill
with glorious gifts of wisdom,
of peace and joy, laughter and loved ones,
I think sometimes I really don't deserve,
and yet You give, in such abundance,
your love to me each and every day.
I pray and ask for Your forgiveness
for my sins, for my transgressions and trespasses,
my wicked thoughts, my inadequacies.

For Thee I live
to sing You, my glorious gracious God,
a fount of ever-flowing praise.
I bend my aching aging knees
and bow my head,
close my tired, teary eyes,
and open my heavy heart to Thee, Sweet Lord.
I am, and forever will be, your servant, striving
to be a better human being,
a humble man worthy of Your love and all these blessings,
a person of pure heart, mind, and soul.
Thank you for every day, Heavenly Father.
It is for Thee I live.

About the Author

Randy D. Rubin lives in quiet lunacy with his dog daughter Eva Larue in a very old haunted house in Virginia. He is a proud member of The Horror Writers of America and HW A-VA. He matriculated from Old Dominion University studying Creative Writing/English. He has two novellas published by Secret Cravings Press, "THE LEGEND OF MY NANA, MISS VIOLA" and "THE WITCH OF DREADMERE FOREST". His short story, "TOMMY KITTY CELLAR SON" is part of the anthology, SUFFER THE LITTLE CHILDREN, published at CRUENTUS LIBRI PRESS and "THIS IS A TROLL FREE CALL" is in UGLY BABIES Vol. I. through JWK Publishing. His story, "THE WATER GOT MAD" is part of Perpetual Motion Machine Publishing's ONE NIGHT STAND series. He is the featured poet showcased in THE HORROR ZINE's September 2014 issue.

He won the NECON E-Book Flash Fiction Contest in 2015 and received an honorable mention for his haiku poetry. His flash fiction took second place in the January 2015 Short Fiction Contest at TheCultofMe.Blogspot.com this year.

His dark passions and prose have been turned into podcasts at THE WICKED LIBRARY, Episodes 417 in 2014 and 516 in 2015 and 613 in 2016. His drabbles have appeared at HELLNOTES Horror in a Hundred. His first dark poetry collection, "The Demon in My Head Doth Speak" was released in February 2015. His short story, "T-BONE" can be enjoyed in the Happy Little Horrors Anthology Vol 2 - ALIENATED at AMAZON. His second poetry collection, "The Joint' is incorporated into "The Prison Compendium", a tome of dark and sinister prison stories and poems which 'broke out' in November 2016.

Find our more at www.dreadmere.com

www.ingramcontent.com/pod-product-compliance
Lightning Source LLC
Chambersburg PA
CBHW060330050426
42449CB00011B/2711